Praise for *O Body*

By the time in *O Body* Sullivan says of his
mine," we're already immersed in the world of a masterful storyteller. The po-
et-speaker of the collection is our guide, narrating a journey bridging two cit-
ies—Chicago, the home he is made of, and Bloomington, the home he makes
and that remakes him. *O Body* is an epic poem for our modern-day, examining
what it means to be a man, assuming the mantle of husband and father. In it,
Sullivan also confronts a subject too little treated by men—self-image tied to
weight, to the body we must learn to live in and love. The voice of this collec-
tion is as profound as it is unassuming: here are timely, piercing odes, cognizant
of loss yet veering always in the direction of praise, gratitude, and awe.
—**Shara McCallum, author of *No Ruined Stone***

Dan "Sully" Sullivan's *O Body* is a feat of tenderness, an act of profound, sweet
wondering, the word I mean is care, not only for the home of one's own body,
but for the homes one's body might offer other bodies. The shelter we might
make of each other. He gets there by going deep with his sorrow and his shame.
He gets there through humor and music and story. And when he emerges, he
brings with him devotion. To a city, a home, a partner, a daughter, all of them
with their own luminous and permanent rooms in this wondrous, this acciden-
tal, this precious, *O Body*.
—**Ross Gay, author of *Be Holding: A Poem***

Sully's work feels to me like some version of Chicago I fell in love with once.
The work is tender and tenderhearted and insecure and imperfect and on the
verge of something truly astounding. I love these poems that speak of a city that
feels like a body: soft even when softness is a liability, hard at the corners, and

complicated as hell. Sully is a special poet but perhaps he is not a special poet but rather a special partner and special tour guide and special food lover and special parent. Maybe, though, all those things are the things that can make a special poet.

—Nate Marshall, author of FINNA

The voice in Sully's book, *O Body*, is intimate and tender—these are tavern style poems to be shared with friends and strangers over beer and pizza. I could tell you about the voltas in these poems, how the language of images builds in the poems and then throughout multiple poems, and it's all true, but mostly, I want you to know I read *O Body* in one sitting. I laughed and gasped and cussed because of how good these poems are.

—José Olivarez, author of *Promises of Gold*

O Body

Dan "Sully" Sullivan

Foreword by Adrian Matejka

Haymarket Books
Chicago, Illinois

Published in 2023 by
Haymarket Books
P.O. Box 180165
Chicago, IL 60618
773-583-7884
www.haymarketbooks.org
info@haymarketbooks.org

ISBN: 978-1-64259-974-9

Distributed to the trade in the US through Consortium Book Sales and Distribution (www.cbsd.com) and internationally through Ingram Publisher Services International (www.ingramcontent.com).

This book was published with the generous support of Lannan Foundation, Wallace Action Fund, and Marguerite Casey Foundation.

Special discounts are available for bulk purchases by organizations and institutions. Please email info@haymarketbooks.org for more information.

Cover artwork and design by Julian Gallo.

Library of Congress Cataloging-in-Publication data is available.

10 9 8 7 6 5 4 3 2 1

Contents

Foreword

Those of us who have been lucky enough to read Sully's previous book, *The Blue Line Home,* already know he's a poet of Chicago. The Chicago of Old Style and hot dogs with tomato and pickle. The tough cadences, the concrete-scraped knees, beats-made-from-fists-and-palms-on-lunchroom-tables Chicago. Everything Michael Jordan and wind that stops you in your tracks the same way the never-ending construction on the Dan Ryan does. The poems sound like they were meant to be read in Soldier Field in lake effect snow. Or maybe they are just so true that their truths would stand up in the elements, the way people who embrace Chicago and are, in turn, embraced by the City of Broad Shoulders must stand up.

Or at least that was the Sully I met in Chicago nine years ago. He was working with Peter Kahn at Oak Park River Forest High School in their incredible Spoken Word Club. I was at the school to lead a workshop and was immediately knocked out by Sully's enthusiasm and generosity. The way he loved the students and the students loved him back. The bigger kindnesses came through in the work the students produced with Sully's guidance. He gave them space to be who they wanted to be on the page. There was a kind of transferable vulnerability in Sully that belied the bigger architectures of performance and bluster so many of us are schooled in as young men.

It's better to be anxious inside and tough on the exterior than to admit uncertainty and have everyone coming for you. That's not a Chicago mantra or spoken word or hip-hop mantra. That's something that most men are presented with as fact. Even in poetry, even in teaching, openness can be a complication. So to see this man who was already aware of the tension created by his presumed masculinity working to make the world around him less full of headbutts and fists was inspiring. I should say *is* inspiring because the work is still ongoing in the empathetic lyricism of this new book, *O Body*.

These tight, masterful poems are fragile and nervous and beautiful as they interrogate the male body, its image, and the privileges affixed to that body, regardless of shape. They recognize the bull-in-a-china-shop momentum men have as they make their way through the world. Belief systems get wrecked, put back together, then wrecked again in these poems. At the same time, the poems sonorously acknowledge that there is a little one right at the edge of the afternoon trying to take a nap. That people in this speaker's life require a body that isn't made in opposition to gravity, one that can be careful and nuanced. The book is a migration narrative: Chicago to Bloomington, first, but also inside the speaker—the self, the body, the family. That's where the true movement resides.

Even when the poems in *O Body* aren't directly about family or fatherhood, they are completely about family and fatherhood. Who Sully is today as a writer is wholly inseparable from who he is as a father and husband. The successes and the failures, all of the moments of joy and wonder: Chicago's blustery ethos is no longer the engine for Sully's poetry. It's been replaced by a kind of tactile symmetry that the Second City couldn't offer. No more Soldier Field, no more Harold's or Margie's or Felony Franks. The apparatus for that kind of living has been dismantled in favor of something more elegant and unexpected, something that makes wonder legible. I've never seen poetry like this before.

—*Adrian Matejka*

The delight alone or in the rush of the streets, or along the fields and hill-sides,
The feeling of health, the full-noon trill, the song of me rising from bed
    and meeting the sun

—*Walt Whitman*

All the crazy wonderful slamming roar of the street—
O God, there's noises I'm going to be hungry for.

—*Carl Sandburg*

1.

The Story Goes Like This:

I'd meet a girl who wore the shade of green that rain looked like.

She tells *this* story:
Out on Ashland Ave outside the Ice Factory,
which sounds like an industrial Chicago landmark or a bar on Rush

but was just a warehouse where five guys threw house parties,
her coat was stolen from behind the old mustard couch. I gave her my down
jacket in the crush of January.

I remember wanting
to kiss her. There ain't a smooth bone in my build but I got it right that night

unless you ask her. I should have lingered
longer on the stone stoop step. I keep telling myself this. I guess
I just wanted to know it was only a first.

We've had touchpoints like these,   landscape
markers that allowed us to plant seeds along street curbs.

Our first date at Pick Me Up Cafe. *Bloodroot.*
Our first kiss outside the Three Arts Club. *Hydrangea.*
Where we first met out on Wabash. *Troutlily.*

A decade passes & our autumn arms empty. We are at the age
where the body's height reverses, begins to move toward earth instead
of branches reaching like hands anxious to be called on.

Our neighbors are screaming
at each other outside our bedroom window. I'm hustled out of sixty bucks
on the el on the way to work. Her car dies. This body
    of the city is less garden to me now & more millions of mouths.

On Looking at My Own Body

I'm built like all my uncles like a football coach like a
football like a couch like a teardrop camper like a yoga
ball like a pink Prius like a pulpit like a poorly assembled
barn like half a Nancy's pizza like a block of cheddar I
look like I smell like a cabin like I just ate your auntie's
Labor Day casserole like I like Seth Rogen movies like a
whole milk latte like I just have to embrace the man
boob like hold myself in the mirror like a mirror is
different than a photo like I don't know if I see what I
want to or need to like I see how I regulate gravity like
gravity loves me too much like damn gravity I need some
space

Bridge Built in the Form of Prayer

High Bridge spreads the width of the river,

rolling over my road like a cellar spider.

I pay to get from home to home. I like to dream it

& scream from entrance to exit—a half-mile

pitch. The Calumet is not an exciting body—

The road home a lull of corn, smog & steel,

holding on upside down. I often think about

what these hands can or cannot do. As a kid,

I built a bridge of sticks from an oak tree.

       It still stands.

there was a floating sidewalk the width of six bodies,

the people bridge. I would crawl out of the basement

with Krylon: seaside, sunrise, satin island, climb

& paint a mural of a bowhead whale

in a blanket-blue sky

          stretching its arms,

          This bridge, a toll

          like a roller coaster

          of truss & high-

          just a hub for industrial ships.

          so what I imagine is

          my open palms–the map of them–

          in my parents' yard,

          That broken pile took root.

          Two blocks from that house,

          we called it

          window. I was wearing a backpack full

          beneath the bridge

          leaping from the doldrum

          & never coming down.

We Always Ate the Kraut Pierogi First

I run the ramp at Cicero, tripping
over my Sauconys & my watch
says I already missed the point.
On a platform ad, somebody tagged
NO CITY CAN BITE YOU.

My plan was to read
The Bean Eaters by Gwendolyn
Brooks on the train. When an
angry mob burns books, I wonder
what they pretend not to know.

It's 8:02 a.m. & I'll be shuffling
into work a half-past-a-stern-talking-to-from-Catherine-in-HR
when up pulls, at Ashland &
the Eisenhower, The North Pole
Express. My blue line train car

decked out like Santa's sleigh.
A six-foot-tall reindeer costume
hands me candy canes like I'm nine
again. Ten stops to work & now I'm all
jolly-like in the Loop like it's not morning,

like I'm not mourning, like Gramma
Adeline's tinsel-ridden tree at 47th
& Whipple still has the lights on or

pierogi from Schli's Deli is still
steaming the length of a table that

has all our folding chairs filling
the space in her kitchen.
Tony with the boat who lived
next door had a dog we called
Pipsqueak. He was seven pounds

packed like snow with the highest
pitched bark, another siren serenade
at Christmas dinner. I never saw
Tony too much but Pipsqueak
had pipes. This was before

Uncle Dave moved to Tampa.
He worked for Rand McNally
& wrapped all of our presents
in road maps, like he knew
we were going somewhere.

Not for Tourists Guide to Chicago #17

Look, the numbers are formality:
call expressways by their names—
Stevenson, Kennedy, Ryan, Ike,
Edens. Jane Addams gotta tollway,
Jane Byrne gotta interchange.
Each street is a festival & they know

how you want your hot dog.
It ain't just about depth in the pan.
You should use the distance
to measure time. Find a preposition
to end a sentence with. Know where
you at. Vowels are flat, laid out

on the stoop. The stoop of the tongue
is stone. Language falls slow from
corners like cinder block. The S
in Illinois is silent. You are not
Chi-rish when you dress green
as a river. Drink   this in, Joe, it's

the Go or Go IL, definitely windy,
still hog butcher, big shoulders but
we don't call it Chai-Town unless
we're in some Wicker Park clever
coffee shop & you know what,
we're not.

Malnati's

Lou had to know it was funny to open an Italian restaurant
in a Jewish neighborhood on St. Patrick's. Even a Comiskey kid
ain't got no problems when Lou's at the plate. As long as
he's around, Payton is still rushing the end zone, Dawson
is at the ivy & Ernie is smiling in the thick of it. Just check
the frames on the wall. I'm telling you, Lou knew to sauce
thick, to fresh hot, to pepperoncini, to bowl shuffle. It begins
every time with that cornmeal crust then finds an end with a fork
& knife. Even Chicagoans know you can't eat this one
with your hands. It wasn't a northside thing. It's just that
no place had the space other than that Lincoln Ave lot
to fit all the cheese he was shoving in that pan. No 37th Street
rowhouse, no live-work 2 flat, no narrow corridor. It just had to
let its belt loose.

Butter was doing a show with his band in Wrigleyville, a weird place to rap,

but that's not the point. I knew Marisa would bring Whitney. Whitney wore
a thrift shop t-shirt with a hippo on it holding a microphone with the caption:

hippo-hop. She'd tell me one day she wore it to impress me. It worked.
I don't know what I wore, but sadly it may have been a fedora & I wish I were

lying. I knew she was a woman I wanted to share tourist stuff with that I didn't do in my
own city. Take her to my uncle's bbq in Bolingbrook for a Mai Tai

& fireworks. Check out some new brewery on Dempster. Rent an apartment
off the e-way in Logan Square where dust from the open windows coated

every surface. Make her an owl-shaped almond cake for her twenty-eighth
birthday. Rent a condo on Monticello & get harassed together by an angry

downstairs neighbor with a broom. Get a grumpy dog named Dilbert & let him chew
through the corner of our beige recliner. Take her to Hot Doug's

for a veggie dog with celery salt. Take her to my brother's wedding in Puerto Vallarta.
Take her to my students' poetry reading. My poetry reading. Take her to see

Nas & Damien Marley in Union Park off the green line. Get a ring for her.
Let her throw out all my fedoras. Marry her on a small lake in Grand Junction.

Buy a bed together that wasn't a futon. Buy a house that smelled & work
on it until it didn't smell & also had floors. Work on it until there was insulation

above the nursery. Until there was a crib & a place to hang a mobile above it.
Until the cracks above the door frames were a sign our house was settling in.

Date Night

Whitney says she has to be in the mood
for it. She says it's sweet & likes it

saucy. She says she can just relax &
let me order, take control. *It's a big deal,*

she says, *for you.* & it really is. She isn't sure
who she is *with* right now, me or the green

pepper & onion butter crust pan pizza.
I don't take just anyone   *here.*

Wave Built in the Form of Prayer

I get this gravity from my mom's side. My father was always thin
& I don't mean to speak of him like he's dead—he's not

thin anymore. I know the earth pulls us closer as we age, but his softer
body does not make me think of tombs. I think of passage & mirrors.

I am most aware of my body when it fails me. On a day we evade
Chicago, head out on a hike with Colin & Angee, I stop to rest

on large rocks & say *I'll catch up* more often than I'd like.
They don't judge me, but I feel the collocated sweat of difference

on my back. My relationship with my body/city has always been
complicated. I am never sure if it is mine. On the southside,

all the corner bars had Old Style signs that read *Zimne Piwo*
which is Polish for "Cold Beer." My cousin Scott came to visit

& said, *This Zimne guy owns a lot of bars around here, huh?*
When I was six, we moved to the first suburb west of downtown.

In high school, the city was an escape. I'd skateboard
at the old Amoco building or hit an open mic off Damen

but always found my way home. I am on the outside & inside
simultaneously. I have stood, sometimes for what was maybe days,

on suburban el-train stops, just trying to get out of the rain.
I try to stand taller than I usually feel. I pull my hands back

behind me & lean forward to open my chest. In yoga, I think
this is called   *stretching*. I swear some days the memory foam

in my mattress remembers it hates me. Say my weight in the mirror
three times & it appears. When does my body stop being a goal?

As a boy I was fluid as a mid-June wave crawling up
North Avenue's   shore, rhythmic   as lip lapping land.

The Best Stories

In first grade, Peter brought a fat
branch down on my neck for slogging
around the first base line. It broke
the skin & wasn't the first time

I blubbered in the grass in front
of everyone. I fixed masking tape
over my nipples before gym
in middle school so they laid flat

in my uniform, did not draw
attention, snickers, or titty-twisters.
Unlike other fat kids that put t-shirts
on to swim in the lake at Montrose,

I never wanted to wear anything
that made me feel heavier.
I'm not sure when I first felt fat.
I do know that my first-grade teacher

told me to pull my shirt down
while reading out loud to the class
because my belly was hanging out.
I don't know how much

I liked school, but I learned.
I also know when Curtis swung
his backpack in circles & hit me
in the head on accident, I broke

his nose. I know rage erupts
from large shadows in my gut.
Even today, as a man taking up space,
my rage is a child I struggle to know

how to hold. I wonder what narratives
we privilege, which get retold, when
it is okay to be fat or angry. I've heard
I was born looking like I had thirty

marshmallows smuggled in my cheeks.
Had toes like ten dumplings.
Fat rolls pinch-ready.
You were a big baby, my mom says

every Christmas. *I still am,* I joke
every Christmas. The best stories
        are round.
They come back to you.

I Went as a Ten-Year-Old Fat Captain Kirk for Halloween

There were no obese main characters on Star Trek so there was hope
I could be the first. At recess, I stared up at the deep sky in left field
in my black sweats & long-sleeve yellow shirt, in the game & not
all at once. In October, even the trees want to wear different skin.
When the inning ended, Brendan yelled *Get off the field, Star Trek!*
I sprinted back to the dugout, startled, head still in the clouds &
without grace, tripped on my own sneaker lace, the side of my face
grinding against blacktop. I used to pretend the bunker under
the back porch could voyage on impulse power to a plump planet
where my weight wasn't measured in mass but some kind of *if*.
I acted as if I didn't care my classmates laughed as long as they did,
joked that I must have eaten too much candy corn on the cob. I just
stood up embarrassed, wiped my cut cheek onto my yellow sleeve &
beamed right along with them.

On Looking at My Own Body

Whitney apologizes for posting a picture of me online without a shirt on as if she anticipates the way I wince when I catch myself on screen. I don't want her to see me feeling unattractive. My coworker, Shane, wears sweats to the office & doesn't bat a lash. They say black is slimming, but it's not my color. I'm more envy or disconsolate. I tailor every pair of flat-front pants I buy. I bet I spend more   time thinking about optical illusions than anyone. My peppered beard lengthens me, makes a road of a molehill. It must be freeing for some folks not to think about their body when they walk into the office or a classroom or a bedroom. There is no easy way to feel uncomfortable. Whoever said *nothing tastes as good as skinny feels* ain't never been to Pierogi Fest in Whiting, Indiana, but I have been   thin & there is something else to feel, too.

2.

Chicago,

I do think about leaving.

It was seven degrees outside with ten inches of lake-effect snow

the April day I was born & you

think you can hold summer over my head

like I don't have a skyline's worth of shade.

Like I don't know that bean downtown is just your cold dead heart.

Like I didn't polar bear my gut through your lake's thin ice in high school.

I swear that's why I still wear all this deep dish.

You still think you can scare me.

Like your winters mean something.

Like I'm not as stubborn as you.

Like your windchill fools somebody.

Like I ain't got this here couch cushion in a parking spot,

Like my dad didn't teach me how to rock a stuck car.

You act like you don't want me.

Like I don't know how to start fires.

Like I can't jury-rig my radiator into a humidifier.

Like I won't stack hoodies on like a one-man sauna.

Like my walls aren't stuffed with insulation.

Like a paycheck in my hands can't stretch.

Like you can wear that vortex & I won't choose to mean mug back.

Like I can't just

leave.

On Looking at My Own Body

Noah said the only reason we celebrate anything is for food. I want to celebrate the body I'm in, but everything that fits has got a letter X on its collar like my framework is taboo. Like I'm at a threshold. Like I'm crossing over. Like I'm an unknown quantity. Am I oversharing when I say that I'm fat? I know you know. I'm just walking & a man on the street works to get my attention, repeats, hey big guy hey big guy. He asks for two bucks & now I'm more aware of my own body than his situation. Point it out & I will think about it. But don't point it out. That's the point. It's like an elephant in my bedroom. Do you assume I spend too much time consuming? This is not about control. I am thinking more about chaos. COWARD & OUTLAW look similar on paper. By chaos, I think I mean perception. By coward, I mean confidence. By outlaw, free. I am a fractal composite of what I think you see. What are you thinking? From where I'm standing, how many shadows I cast depends on how much light there is.

Not for Tourists Guide to Chicago #36

Hot Doug's closed, but you can order jalapeño sausage at Fulton Market. If you're near O'Hare, go to Jean & Jude's. They put the fries right on it. But stay in the city. Go to Duks on Ashland. The blue line is the closest el & your legs will be tired. Mine are. Go to Pete's Red Hots on Roosevelt Rd. Go to O'Malley's in Bridgeport. Maxwell Street just for kicks. Keep some napkins on you. Maybe even an extra shirt. The first Harold's is on 37th & King Drive, but any Harold's will do. If they have pizza on the menu, leave. Go to a different one & by a different one, I mean the one on 87th St. Portillo's is good, but they're too big now. If you do go, get a cake shake. Combo. Hot giardiniera. If you want a malt, go to Margie's or Tastee Freeze on 43rd. There's always Felony Franks on Western if you take the bus. They might be closed now. Hollywood Frank's if you've got a car. If it has Frank in the name, you're good. If you want a pizza puff, hit Nicky's on Pulaski. What's a pizza puff, you ask? What does it sound like? Chicken & Waffles for Chicken & Waffles. Lem's for BBQ. The tamales on Cermak or from Danny's or Rainbow on Division out of the tamale guy's lunchbox. Al's Beef for sure. On Taylor. Or Johnnie's on North. Soul Vegetarian for soul vegetarian. Lao Sze Chuan in China Town when it's cold out. Phở Việt in Little Vietnam with a bubble tea. Parthenon for sit-down Greek if you need to sit down. You'll need to sit down. Greek Islands for riganati. Czech Plaza in Berwyn. Polish Highlanders on Archer for kielbasa but Podhalanka in West Town for pierogi. Gyro or Vice Lord burger on Madison, your choice. Prime Butt at Schaller's Pump. J.J. Fish. 90 Miles for masas de puerco. Manny's Deli for corned beef. Bagel Country for bagels. Salt & Pepper, Hollywood Grill, Ann Sather's, Golden House, any diner really. MacArthur's on the Westside for dessert. Taco Burrito King, Lalos, Mi Tierra, La Pasadita, Nuevo León, Cemitas Puebla, Garcia's, Maria's, El Típico, El Tapatio & El Barco. Sultan's Market in Wicker Park or Pita Inn on Dempster but just know that no one here takes the purple line.

Michael Jordan's Mansion in Chicago Is Still on the Market

Van Gundy said Jordan was your best friend off-court
so he could catch you off guard come game time. Barkley
said Mike's casino seat was always taken; he knew to bet
on himself. Were those two years in baseball a ploy

to avoid suspension? His debt, his father,
his father's death. *There is an I in win* Mike would
tell you. The microphones weren't close enough
to catch him on court. He would back off 5'3"

Muggsy Bogues say, *Shoot it, you fucking midget.*
Jordan took shots at his friends in his hall of fame
acceptance speech, barely even mentioned Pippen.
Before you'd get crossed over or he caught you

sleeping at the buzzer, he'd get in that head, had
words for you, that trash talk, that ice-cold, that
nineteen-footer, that free throw with his eyes
closed. Muggsy missed by a mile. Michael would

shake & bake with Bugs Bunny. Dance on Saturday
Night Live with Da Superfans in a hula skirt.
He'd dunk from your free throw line, the sideline
of your shoe, the tag on your shirt, the screen

at your local IMAX, his tongue hanging
from the rim of his lip. Your preacher would

use him as a metaphor during Sunday sermon.
Your aunt would swoon, *How handsome.* You had

his rookie card framed. Muggsy's shot never did
recover but you cried when Michael got that Olympic
gold, kissed his mother's forehead & placed it
around her neck.

Whitney laughs at my dad joke about carrots[*] & immediately is mad that she did because it was so dumb.

I can hear myself from the outside when I've raised my voice like a bad song
caught between stations. I've put a dumb fist through a clothes hamper.
I'm working on it in therapy. So when I hear a joy that erupts, too much
for wit or vascular organ, I hold close that movement of feeling between hurt
& love. I wonder what our first was? Some goof-word knocking

from our tongues? The release, an audible blush, cognitive & spontaneous.
Maybe it was a poor choice at Blockbuster on Harlem Ave. Something starring Stephen
Baldwin. My burnt pancakes? You know what I mean. We flip them
into something that leaps. Each laugh that lives between us is a touch, mouths
that close & draw & open like a bridge that connects two sides of the river.

---

[*] If you must know, when I pulled a carrot from the drawer in the fridge, I mumbled to myself,
Now where's that snowman…

Not for Tourists Guide to Chicago #29

Look, there are contracts to fix all the sidewalks on the Gold Coast.
There is a bean with your face on it, not mine. Chicago is a body beaten
with random acts of legislation, a persistent series of band aids &
I can afford to live in the center of it. What I'm saying is, I was born
in a hospital that doesn't exist anymore. That empty lot sits on Division
between brownstones & fire escapes in the shadow of my grandma's
house. I have wanted to fill the space. It's not an address or memory,
but up close, my own full face in puddles like a mirror of how I begin.
Look, I'm trying to reckon with how this city is built to protect people
like me while I still feel so angry. Yes, you can be from here and not
in the same breath. Yes, this is part of the tour. What do I want
you to know? I don't need warmth. I mean I want to remember.
I mean I want to belong, cradled in debris.

What Stays

+a shout out to Robert Hayden

On Whipple, it took one open window to cover everything in dust.
In our first apartment together off the expressway, it was best to wake early

before rush hour. We'd let the previous night escape before the college kids above
or the flight attendant below spent all the hot water. When my buddy

Adam came to visit us on Lawndale, our second place, he said *Damn Sully,*
this apartment adult as hell. I guess it was. We hung art we bought

with our own money & had a pot-rack over the kitchen island. The floors
were oak but walls were like screen doors that let the outside in & we weren't

ready to have the whole neighborhood with us at breakfast. At our place
on Monticello, we finally could open windows when our neighbors barbequed

so that we could hear the laughs of children on the block like distant ghosts
we didn't know we needed. Whitney planted thyme & hyssop

in the side yard & the aphids ate them. The hallways could swallow us whole
but we couldn't find the source of hollow air in the spare room, the austere

& lonely office it was. It was close. We had all the right red rugs & plush throws
to make it home, but had to have known we were just renting time.

They are calling at dinner on the day before the deadline

& Whitney will be home from work any minute &

they say I got into the graduate program &

I know that by leaving Chicago she's got more to lose

because, I mean, I don't lose family by moving further from them,

I just am further from them, but

I'm still there if that makes sense &

I had all but given up on this school &

I was tired of loving a city

with fists, but also our living room right now where I sit

casts light over her grandmother's cherry hutch &

it really does look gorgeous &

there's a stick in the bathroom waste bin with a pink line on it &

they tell me about what craft courses they offer &

the benefits of a small cohort & I know we'll lose health insurance &

I do not want to resent a job or the skyline that raised me & the pedagogical

component of the program sounds quite promising &

I did call this my Walter Payton year since he wore 34

but I say that mostly to hide my fear of anything after this &

I really hate to let anyone know I'm scared, let alone my wife &

there will be one weekend to find a place to live &

our daughter is due in November &

we will name her after a family member I have never met &

we will have to buy a house on short notice because

it's more affordable than renting there somehow &

it would be a wreck & stocky like me but cute &

I can hear Whitney with her keys at the back door now &

I wouldn't be sure which walls are load bearing

or how it would stand but it would &

on our first day there a waitress at a diner nearby

would tell us her favorite thing about tornadoes

in Indiana is seeing where everything lands.

On Looking at My Own Body

Some truck stop in September with a burger joint on its side & I'm wet from the rain & I ask this old-timey photo of a man for directions to Fair Oaks Farms & he said I don't believe there's any way from here to there & I take that with me all the way into days like this where my legs are other cities like Chicago in the summer & I never really get where I'm going so I let my legs know it's fine if they hate hikes & wet thigh jeans & uneven sidewalks to an old red chapel I'm supposed to see in the daylight & it's fine if they just need to sit down for a second because not ever getting there takes a lot longer than you might think.

3.

Watch:

after Nikki Patín

how, on your way in, the sweats you wear to meet unspoken dress codes draw glances.

how lobby small talk makes their eyes flit from your face to your shoulder to behind you,

how you might not even get that, like there's someone more important on the room's horizon.

how they see through you, despite any amount of body you have.

how people side-eye you on the treadmill then look away, quick.

how some guy opts for the next aisle over in the locker room like fat is infectious.

how your face undoes itself when it finally reaches the bathroom mirror.

how your shoulders unclench from their perceptive coils.

how you breathe when alone in your thoughts.

how your jaw eases when you get off your tenterhooks.

how sudden & easy it is to step out knowingly under the halogen.

how the water responds when your toes hit the empty pool.

how your gentle touch quakes the stillness.

how it ripples out like translucent skin.

how your legs course then surge.

how the right one swishes then ruptures the surface.

how the left follows & makes a game of each movement.

how even as your goggles fog you see your length: slick & full of grace.

how the lap markers move further & further from you.

how your bicep slips under smooth & forearm dips into the gradual deep.

how you push the water away & it still envelops you.

how powerful it is to move what feels unmovable.

how your hand slides down your side slick, back up & forward.

how it repeats. how it recurs. current. recurrent. repeat. repeat. repeat.

how it is just you, amassing the air you need.

how it is just you.

how everything here must move & then return.

O Body

But what of the body when it is not a pinnacle?
When it is benched, belching, retaining water
like a dam or a teeming pink pot? When you, body,
lumber your way from point B to A, not broken

but o, so tired, so full of breakroom coffee,
know that the reflection near the lighthouse
on a heavy shore is still yours. You might not
know how to let your guard down. I have slept

for what has felt like days, too. O dry-skinned,
wavering body, I know you might need some lotion,
but whatever. Let this be your stillness. That's
what I can do. Be your reflection, your you,

without a rippling wave. Light up the dark
& freckled night with your fullness. O manboob,
o sunburnt farmer, some days you can install
a ceiling fan all on your own, standing your big ass

on the most rickety chair in the house & get away
unscathed, but tonight, body, I can't promise
you'll be a whole-note moon, name you wolf,
wildflower, wavellite. I still need you to know

you are worthy of every moon that reminds you
of you. I admit I can't always think of a love song.

Some days, I have to put you on shuffle. Some days,
body, you spend an extra seven minutes

on the toilet to avoid work emails. You snag that
second walnut muffin from a free continental motel
breakfast. O body, you reheat spaghetti in holiday
Tupperware & stand the way everyone does

in an elevator: front-facing & defeated. O, body,
your annoying knee bounces under the table
until someone, under breath, breathes out *God.*
Stop. O, God. O, good body, some days you are

just okay & that's okay. It is all you need to be.
I have been there when you kickflipped down
that set of stairs on the Lincoln School playground
& landed the hell out of it. I filled your lungs

with air & watched you hurl it toward stage lights
in a Hamburg theater. I love you just the way you are.
Call me Fred Rogers. I will call you Tiger. Daniel,
don't you feel forgotten. Take up space.

Take your time. You are more than just adjacent.
O Body, marooned & frustrated, sure,
maybe you should cut your nails even though
it's only been like a week & a half but I'm still here

with you. You are fine and I don't mean it like okay.
I mean it like *damn*. O body, o gentle, luscious oaf.
O, scorekeeper. O, you big, lovely history book.
You are one loyal animal. I know you can sweat out

a last Grant Park lap in June or even two-step to Etta
under a North Lake Michigan moon. I have lived it
with you. We love to dance when the mood strikes
us at just the right angle. O, heavy angel. O, sweat

lodge. O, full belly, woah, nelly. You don't have to
be a moon or an ocean, body, because from where
I'm standing, the lake upon which your reflection sets
feels endless.

Upon TSA Confiscating My Norelco Beard Trimmer

Every *thing* has violence in it. Oh, this dangerous

    tool of my body. What butchery do you

imagine to your necks? Just think

    what my aftershave might do. What unstrung

shoelace hasn't thought of becoming

    a choke chain? My water bottle can trigger

a full-fledged investigation,

    teeth on a hoodie's zipper can rip

the silent attention of an executive

    reading in an aisle seat, a broken arm

from this pair of glasses can stab

    the canvas of a carry-on from its insides. And yet,

I am entitled to this grievance, so rip the stub

    from the white slab of my boarding pass.

You concentrate on everyone else. Turn them into clickbait

headlines in your mind while I wait

& wait in your line. My belt slips

slow from my waist. I hold it in two

fists, pull it taut, then relax & watch

it curve, so familiar, into a routine smile.

April Is National Celery Month

Celery tastes like grasswater

you can snap. You know

the old jingle: *snap some grasswater*

in your mouth. People who say

cheese curds are overrated

are the same that think

celery is a snack. It's not

good. It means nothing

to your body. Celery is the grossest

placebo. You may ask: *but what*

about antioxidants? & I will answer

you: *Yes. What about them?*

This isn't some fat guy

rant about how real men eat

cheeseburgers. I'm pescatarian

& carrots are my jam. I can go

ham on some brussels sprouts.

This isn't a metaphor. It isn't

about how something can feel

like nothing, how bright

& crisp emptiness can be.

It's about celery &

how much

I hate it.

On Looking at My Own Body

There is a swamp in me. An agitated sludge for sure. Banana first, unsalted almonds, a fist of greens, chia seeds, pineapple chunks, coconut milk & that Greek yogurt from Aldi. I have to time it so that I can start the blender before O's 9 a.m. nap, lift one to my lips now & slug one for lunch before the content settles & gets as thick as I feel in the reflection of a passing window. Spinach green fades banana brown swishing inside my backpack by 1 p.m. 5 days a week. 10 smoothies for 10 meals. 14 months in & 17 pounds down since leaving Monticello Ave to follow winding back roads to here. 45 seconds of knee-repeaters then Russian twists then low-impact burpees, repeat in a house with warped floorboards & walls that shake during scotties & jumping jacks. I hold my chest high but feel it all buckle when I enter my classroom & an 18-year-old student with a Ryan Lochte face & performance fleece sees my shake & assumes it's whey. He pushes out I know YOU aren't lifting as if I needed my own student pointing to my body with his words first thing on a Tuesday. No matter how much better this baby blue button-down fits than it did a week ago, language can always shape itself into funhouse mirrors.

The map falls out of our glove box & begins questioning our life choices.

You have to trace the lines & pages will open like a peacock

in bluster. Take this as a dare. It is   what people

did before GPS, read   pink & spidering varicose

places we've never been. You think you are more than

static. You think your feet aren't landlocked. What if

you were more train than fault line? What if your feet

were ships & they knew how to land somewhere   new?

What if you were seasickness then sea legs then sea lion?

There is always something to leave   in a Chicago parking

spot, but there are no dibs. Even old haunts won't look like

home: your dentist's white office, your parents' shotgun

bungalow, just blotch, coarse blood, unfamiliar. You know

you've really moved from a strip mall to a place that feels

like a different strip mall. Even if you think you've spent

too much time on highways stuffing gas station food

into your trap, you wouldn't know to sleep on a bed

that wasn't crafted by the traffic of your worry.

In Pilsen, in a brown brick three-flat apartment, in a front room

that I thought needed me, I'm not sure how to stay.
I'm good at leaving   myself here
in piles of laundry that smell like sidewalk salt.

Here, in remnants of stanzas about ferver & public transit I've left
pinned to a corkboard since September without touch. Here,
where the lake effect makes making it anywhere a prayer. So long to get to here.

I'm dropping in the alley those memories wrapped in plastic like a worn mattress.
The dirt. The traction. The leaving. Soon, I will mop the apartment's sapwood floors.
The windows with the parking lot view will remain open, airing out. Today is a home

I have not taken the time to make. Today,
it is more than what I've allowed.

There Is No Other Word for Touch

When you love a man, he becomes more than a body.
—Gwendolyn Brooks

There is no word for skin that does what touch can do when
you, my love, find me halved in night, hands as if drawing water. You
might think wildfire or stone or chalk or even cumulus, but I love
that skin is only skin when we touch & before is just a

distance we move around a room. In the harbor of your arms, man
is more than an empty vessel adjective or a noun that can breathe.
I disappear to piece tomorrow together in lists but that becomes
I & only present when you are tangible & we are more

than language that folds in on itself & more than
just a word for what flesh does. I love you for this & this is how we intimate a
touch to fettle to no words to apart to liminal to body to hold to body.

& I Can Find a Home There, Too.

When mom lost some of her hearing, the noise of traffic & city
buses at the curb out front drove forward from the backdrop

of our minds & pulled up at our dinner table in Brighton Park,
house on the corner of 42nd & California. I Went to Peace

Lutheran for kindergarten & missed the crossing guard when
she was hospitalized after a hit & run. We moved to Oak Park,

first suburb west of the city. It was a lot closer to downtown
but that city limit speaks volumes. In the fifties, they built

cul-de-sacs all down Austin Ave at the edge of town. It was less
about holding & more about keeping out. Ludacris & Hemingway

both went to my high school. Not at the same time. I guess
I'm asking who gets to speak for the city. I lived in Chicago

more years than anywhere else but what is mine to hold,
if anything. There are seventy-seven neighborhoods & I've had apartments

in fourteen of them. *Starving artist* sounds more romantic
in a Chicago accent than *pioneer of gentrification*. I might as well

have been born a new Humboldt Park brunch spot
next to Luquillos Barber Shop. Maybe I thought I was part

of the landscape. Some urban pastoral entanglement
that connected me to place. Where am I even from.

Rakim said, *it ain't where you from, it's where you at*
& Edward Sharpe said, *home is wherever I'm with you.*

Our CD player doesn't work so Whitney & I flip radio stations
when driving between Illinois & Indiana. I lean more toward

a Rakim ethos. I don't even think Edward Sharpe is one person
but I do think he's white. So what truth I can live in. Chicago

was never mine. That doesn't mean I can't love it. It does mean
I can leave. It means there is another landscape

    & I can find a home there, too.

4.

On Looking at My Own Body

Let's see if we get there. How many times have I asked friends of mine to visit, drive from Chicago through Indiana to me on unlit, narrow roads without thinking of what it's like for them? When I drive that drive, I get to turn up the radio, at ease with the expanse where wind turbines stand in long rows & light in unison. One second the flat horizon blinks red, then darkness. I've named that stretch *Indiana Borealis*. I've even pulled off I-65 on my way from Chicago & walked into a cornfield for the hell of it. I could disappear here. Did you know not all whales have teeth? Jonah was lapped into an echoing stomach. Waves swallow fishermen all the time & go unnoticed.

To Give in to Possibility Is the Hardest Thing

At home in Bloomington, there is a bird's nest
in the mailbox. There's also poison ivy in the carport.
This is not a metaphor. These are just more things
to avoid. Or fix. Anything to distract from the sound
of oxygen in this neonatal recovery unit. Grandpa
mowed over the raspberry bushes Whitney just
planted. This might be a metaphor. I need
to get to class on time but can't leave
until after my daughter's chest x-ray. It feels like
the only thing I can trust is sleep & my wife
would be mad if she heard me say that. That's
a joke. The surgeon wears a red-setting sun on
his scrub hat—it looks like it's from Global Gifts
but I imagine he might have gotten it from some
family that needed someone with hands like his
as much as we need them now. He talks
with them, his hands, I watch
& try to find a metaphor there, too.

I Had Only Ever Heard the Word in Chicago:

persimmon. But in this small town, the word
falls from every branch. My professor invites me
to skateboard. We're old but not that old.

The clouds are plump & still & still here. I am
between classes, cities, trips to Riley Children's
hospital, moments with my daughter.

We skate down Prospect Hill, the centrifuge
separates me from time. We stop by the park
to skate the basketball courts & along the way

he plucks one. His teeth allow pulp to run off
his thumb. I am part concrete, part locomotive.
This is good, he says. When a persimmon isn't

ready yet, it's like chewing on chalk. It puffs your
cheeks. Not like a chipmunk's—more like when
you're listening but just don't know what to say.

...all around us.

Pick me up & throw me into the sea & it will become calm.
  –Jonah 1:12

My arms don't want to leave from her. I feel like an ambulance

hits me when the doctors roll our newborn on a cart, incubated,

around the corner & out of our line of vision. Taking is only one kind

of rupture. We just   wait. This is the only living we can do now.

The only roar we hear is in the stomach. Everything holy in our loneliness.

The waiting room closes in then out. Time is on the outside, moving

in waves, but we are in the darkness. I wonder what Jonah prayed for

other than returning. We anticipate   scars. Our daughter's life

is in the breaking, the water. The break is

House Built in the Form of Prayer

When the divine arrives, stay off Facebook. It's the God of history after all.
The one that is word, then flesh. Yes, fish are common metaphors. I know
what is more important: how the bread breaks. How to need. How the house
on Howe is built. How there may be mold in the crawlspace. How drywall
cracks at the seams. How the foundation shifts. Yes, he walked on water.
He is the God of lakes, too. Of toilets. Of a sink stacked with bowls & butter knives. Of
mildew. Of the lawn that needs water. Of the daughter who hates sleep.
Of old Indiana copper pipes. Yes, the cross. The God of the broken rocking chair.
Of the parts that ship from China & won't arrive for three weeks.
Of my wife hunched, nursing on an ottoman until I fix something, for once.
Of arguing over childcare, or shoes off at the door. Of things I damn well know
how to construct. Yes, there was Jairus' daughter raised from death, perhaps.
The gospels can't agree. She died. Or she was simply sick. Jesus turned toward her in the
crowd. Or he entered her house. The crowd almost crushed him. Or
only his disciples followed. We know she was healed. Her mother is never
mentioned. She is assumed but has no name. Her daughter has no name.
Mostly, I know of all the sons he healed: the official's boy in Galilee, the widow's
in the book of Luke, then lepers, the deaf & blind. What miracles does Jesus do
for our daughters? I know what mothers do. I know the praise of strangers when I walk
the walk of grocery aisles with my daughter strapped in the cart—
what a good dad I must be, how present. How invisible it is when my wife shops for the
same meals. How I haven't even said her name yet. What happens
when I say her name? What little feat to be seen by man. How often does
the bible use the word mother? What sacrifice. How do I use the word?
How is mother used? What answer. What saving grace. What act of noticing.

I just want to be fierce for our daughter,

my wife says through the pulse
of wiper blades while a ceiling
of rainclouds birth against

our windshield. I hold in my hand
the steering wheel halfway
between Cincinnati, Ohio

(our second opinion) & Bloomington,
Indiana, a place that has our home in it.
We've worked to make

our tiny frame anything
opposite a hospital: a welcome
of Antique Rose, Winter in Paris,

soft blankets, the blitt of crickets
through a screen window,
a place where we never stop

staying. No bleating machines
or strange voices. There are security
alarms on doors, homeowner's

insurance, signals of sanctuary
for our neighbors, but we look
at the word differently now: *safety.*

I wish our daughter didn't have to
survive before anything else.
We do what we must to feel normal,

to dust, to meal plan, to paycheck.
We hold back & breathe
through teeth when strangers say

She's so tiny!
while her heart does all the work
it can before the hospital comes

to her again. People instinctively
put a hand over their own heart
when they ask about hers. I wonder

if this is a salute or form of protection.
Everyone has a parallel narrative,
a colloquialism uttered out loud

to move themselves closer
to us. This is what mouses
from people when they don't know

what to say. All our newborn
has ever known is the strength
it takes to live. The doctors say surgery

is the first step & I think of her first steps.
They say the body will do the rest
& I wonder what rest will mean

for her. I look down at my own hands,
trace along the coke-bottle
glass braid that runs the length

of my left palm, brush it against
the barback scar that left my ring finger
nerves numb. This is the body I have—

swelling veins bluing the surface of my calf,
extra flesh pushing tight the buttons
on a dress shirt. It is what it can do—

be some sort of barrel to sleep on.
The only arms I have are open
but what do I know

of the real work a body must do?
When Whitney began labor, it was as if
she already knew what was

on the other side of the blood: the first
time O would wrap her fist,
the size of cotton ball, around a ring finger,

the surreality of walking in
our front door just in time for a first
Christmas after having lived her first

month in a hospital, follow-ups, more
follow-ups, forty miles between home
& hospital each week, her laugh

& her laugh & her joy bursting from
the back aisle during Sunday sermon,
but all I see in front of me is a hospital bed

with all of my love between
its handrails, the rise of Whitney's
heaving breast. I can still feel

the grace of it against the room,
her fingers gripping mine, sheer will & there
is my wife that brought a daughter to us

& there is our daughter screaming
the world onto her, all amniotic fluid
& fury & how a woman's body moves

when there is life & there is life.

Placeholder Built in the Form of Prayer

Seven days ago, a traveling preacher asked us in a strip mall
Starbucks if we could feel Christ's fire in his fist, feel it transmit

into our daughter. What could we say. I do not know   where healing
comes from, what unnameable peace, atlas of scars, body &

the body, the ghosts, holy & holy & holy. What is unseen.
There was snow snapped tight like bedsheets around waiting   room

windows the last time we were here. It is easy to talk   about
weather, fill air inside a mountain   of minutes. What is immovable.

Can you count the number of doors you have   locked   or turned,
times you have held your own   tears in your hands, cupped gently

the weight   of your head as if when raised   from the depth, some
persistent light would open in front of you. Offer up this upholstered

chair, this black coffee, this cafeteria three-cheese panini, this wall
-mounted tv, this pundit, this headline, this nurse that updates us

on the hour, this update, this moment   alone   with my
wife in the lactation room. What should I say   in this prayer. What

distance do I have   to offer. There is another room with our daughter
open   toward a lifetime   of opening. Here, in this glass room of tapping

fingers & grandparents & cross-stitch & magazine racks, I am heaving
myself at the present   nervous-kneed, junk snack, watch watch & pacing.

How could anyone not   hate this. Can't a waiting room be just
a placeholder for hope. I should address the snow. The blizzard kept us

from seeing anything, so I can hold onto this: out the window, this time,
is a courtyard walking toward us, green   so green   so green.

Helminthophobia

after A Disputacioun Betwyx þe Body and Wormes

They made their way through Socrates
& Shakespeare, Da Vinci & Elvis, Freddy
Mercury & Oliver Tambo, my great

grandmother Agnes & your uninspired
Uncle Dean. The bible is silent on Eve's age
when she died so we know what is certain:

the worms ate history. I am sure there is a word
for the fear of worms. When they come for me,
I will not be afraid. I will know the act only

as intimacy. Unless, somehow, I combust
or drown, they will synthesize the current
tender pear of my body to land. We are

a feast at death. We blame Eve for severing us
from Eden, but the flesh of her mouth
joined the apple's skin & united the body

with a promise of potential. Who wouldn't
want to die this way? More than the red
fruit on her curious lip, the worms gift us

separation & harmony all at once. Medieval
studies tell us Homunculi are little genderless
bodies pulled out at death from the mouth.

They cull the soul from worldly joy.
All I'm saying is there is more at work here.
Yes, I think the body can be a joy.

I saw a meme that read *Most people*
will never know how great your body
is meant to feel. Yes, it was a yoga meme.

Am I *most people*? The worms would
never do that to me—put me on one side
of a fence. They only integrate. But can we

think of the body as just a body, read it
without a soul? Is it odd for the body to think
about the body? The body is talking.

Adam lived for one hundred thirty years
& yet, in the end, I am sure the worms,
like God palming the rib, made use.

On Looking at My Own Body

       Would it be too much   to call these stretch marks

a map?

       Too much to connect the dots

       into the shape of

              yes?   Or conjure constellations?

           Too much

      to think of the sun

      then cancer   then Aries   then fire?

                   Too much to ignore the mirror?

      Or befriend it? To pretend

skin means something   more than skin?

           Too much to know there is not too much

                       of me. It is not too much

to watch these rivers flood across my stomach & feel

                           the earth

                  is nothing without its oceans.

I don't know how to use sundials, but I appreciate that shadows have things to tell us

Whitney hates that the watches I wear are dead.
It is always 3:13 when I wear the woodgrain.
Her grandfather was a man with watches.
It was a different time. The magnet around
the earth just ain't what it used to be.

Someone told her I'm a *different kind of dude,*
a good dude, but a different kind of dude. It is
10:47 when I don the brown leather. I ordered
batteries online but they died, too. They always do.
The thing about time is that it's all about

how you wear it. It is 1:29 when I wear navy.
In April, the walk to work is the same length
it takes for three ice cubes to melt in my blue water
bottle. In December, they don't melt
but I'm rarely late & this left wrist

looks good. Why can't I remember what year
my dog died? I named him JJ after Jesse James.
My sister says her boyfriend found a J
in white fur on our dog's chest.
It's true, the J was there but

it doesn't account for the second.
I was in fourth grade when my grandma, Adeline,

died. I rarely remember years, but I can tell you
there are ninety-six stairs up to the third floor at work.
sixteen for each half-flight. I can make it

through *You Are My Sunshine* twice before
I reach the top step. I need to sing it three times
before my daughter naps in my arms. Grandma
always let me stay up past bedtime to watch
M*A*S*H. It was in her sleep. It was 1991.

Once Upon a Time

I apologize for this lengthy email. Whitney & I have had an ongoing discussion about O's "princess" & "ballerina" phase & I wanted to let you in on where we're at. Mostly, in short, we're asking that you help us limit the amount of princessy clothes & toys this Christmas. There are hazardous aspects of "princess culture"—namely that it is an economical machine that targets young girls & enforces dangerous stereotypes. While I get that Belle is independent & reads books, the message that if she is just sweet & gentle to the Beast, he'll become a prince kind of breaks my heart.

*

O turned three   two weeks ago.

It is not lost on us that *this* is what worries us now. If only we always
had the privilege of worrying about how our daughter will rule her kingdom.

I was in Nepal this time last year at Thrangu Tashi Yangtse when Whitney called me
from an Indiana cardiologist's office. She repeated the doctor's words slowly,

It's time to worry about normal parenting stuff.

On Wednesday, O is Cinderella. She puts on cat socks we bought at Target
& calls them glass slippers.

On Thursday, she is Goldilocks and tries Whitney's veggie chili, then
mine, before settling back into her own.

Today, she is a ballerina named Clara and tells us she threw her shoe
at the mouse king & her journey, well, it was all a wonderful dream.

Proximity in the Form of Prayer

I can't promise
every trauma is
a turned stone.
If there are still

secrets that live
in my body, like
little parasites,
they hide, even

from me. I can't
promise to love
myself in every
morning mirror.

In Chicago,
clouds wrapped
their sinewy arms
around buildings

like mourning
families. Here,
we can see stars
from our yard.

When O spots
the moon in

the afternoon,
sunning itself,

unafraid to
follow us home,
we know we are
cumulus, heaping,

touching. This
is where my body is
home in itself,
with you, daughter,

with you, wife.
    I am here.

Acknowledgments

This book is for O and A, who are an unmeasurable source of joy and learning. For Whitney, without whom this book, among so many other things, is not possible. The three of you have my heart, always. Thank you to my parents, siblings, in-laws, and your families for your encouragement and love.

I want to give special thanks to Peter Kahn, my friend and mentor. David Gilmer, Asia Calcagno, Langston Kerman and my OPRF fam. Hannah Brattesani, Franny Choi, Hanif Abdurraqib, Nathaniel Tabachnik, and Rachel Sonis. Shara McCallum, for your kind reflections. Tim "Slam Margera" Stafford, Joel Chmara, Molly Meacham, Robb Q. Telfer, JW Basilo, Shelley Elaine Geiszler, and Marc Kelly Smith, you already know.

Adrian, your friendship, advocacy, and guidance have challenged me to grow as a writer and as a man. Ross, thanks for welcoming me onto your front porch to talk life and poems, and for the potato seeds. To my coho, Wendy, Anni, Essence, Irene, Hannah, Soo Jin and Gionni. Shout out to Brianna Best for taking extra time with these poems. To Stacey, Cathy, Samrat, Romayne, Bob, Shannon, Patricia, Rebekah, Nicholas, Bev, and the rest of my IU folks. To my Bloomington Poetry Slam family, thank you. Thank you to Christine Arthur, Team Body Project, Sonya Renee Taylor, and The Body is Not an Apology for helping me through the journey toward a more radical love for myself, and in turn, others.

My sincere gratitude to Haymarket Books for believing in this collection. Maya Marshall, thank you thank you thank you. This book also wouldn't have been possible without Nate Marshall, José Olivarez, CM Burroughs, Lisa Fishman and Tony Trigilio. Julian Gallo, your friendship and your work on the beautiful cover of this book are everything to me.

Thank you to *Guernica Magazine, Chicago Reader, Rattle, Habitat, The Golden Shovel Anthology, Respect the Mic: Celebrating 20 Years of Poetry from a Chicagoland High School,* and *The View From Here: Stories About Chicago Neighborhoods* for publishing earlier iterations of poems from this collection.

To my Chicago family: Urban Sandbox, Homeroom, Voice of the City, Elastic Arts, Guild Complex, YCA, and all the organizations and venues that held space for young people to share their voices with the world. Thank you. To all the educators and mentors who have held me down all these years: thank you. I hope I'm doing right by you.

About the Author

Dan "Sully" Sullivan holds an MFA and MA from Indiana University. His poems and performances have been featured on HBO Def Poetry Jam, WGN Morning News, and National Public Radio. Sully is a three-time Chicago Poetry Slam Champion, a recipient of the Gwendolyn Brooks Open Mic Poetry Award, the Earl S. Ho Award for Excellence in Teaching Creative Writing, and an Indiana University Writer in South Asia Recipient. His poems have appeared in *Guernica Magazine, Rattle Magazine,* the *Chicago Reader,* and *The Golden Shovel Anthology: New Poems Honoring Gwendolyn Brooks.* Sully is coeditor of the anthology *Respect the Mic: Celebrating 20 Years of Poetry from a Chicagoland High School* (Penguin Random House, 2022) and author of *The Blue Line Home* (EM Press, 2016).

About Haymarket Books

Haymarket Books is a radical, independent, nonprofit book publisher based in Chicago. Our mission is to publish books that contribute to struggles for social and economic justice. We strive to make our books a vibrant and organic part of social movements and the education and development of a critical, engaged, and internationalist Left.

We take inspiration and courage from our namesakes, the Haymarket Martyrs, who gave their lives fighting for a better world. Their 1886 struggle for the eight-hour day—which gave us May Day, the international workers' holiday—reminds workers around the world that ordinary people can organize and struggle for their own liberation. These struggles—against oppression, exploitation, environmental devastation, and war—continue today across the globe.

Since our founding in 2001, Haymarket has published more than nine hundred titles. Radically independent, we seek to drive a wedge into the risk-averse world of corporate book publishing. Our authors include Angela Y. Davis, Arundhati Roy, Keeanga-Yamahtta Taylor, Eve L. Ewing, aja monet, Mariame Kaba, Naomi Klein, Rebecca Solnit, Mohammed El-Kurd, José Olivarez, Noam Chomsky, Winona LaDuke, Robyn Maynard, Leanne Betasamosake Simpson, Howard Zinn, Mike Davis, Marc Lamont Hill, Dave Zirin, Astra Taylor, and Amy Goodman, among many other leading writers of our time. We are also the trade publishers of the acclaimed Historical Materialism Book Series.

Haymarket also manages a vibrant community organizing and event space in Chicago, Haymarket House, the popular Haymarket Books Live event series and podcast, and the annual Socialism Conference.

Also Available from Haymarket Books

Printed in the USA
CPSIA information can be obtained
at www.ICGtesting.com
JSHW051951301123
52937JS00004B/5